READ ON YOUR

W9-BZD-701

Eye on the Sky

CONTENTS

 NATIONAL GEOGRAPHIC

 Hampton-Brown

School Publishing

Words with **ar**

ar

Look at each picture. Read the words.

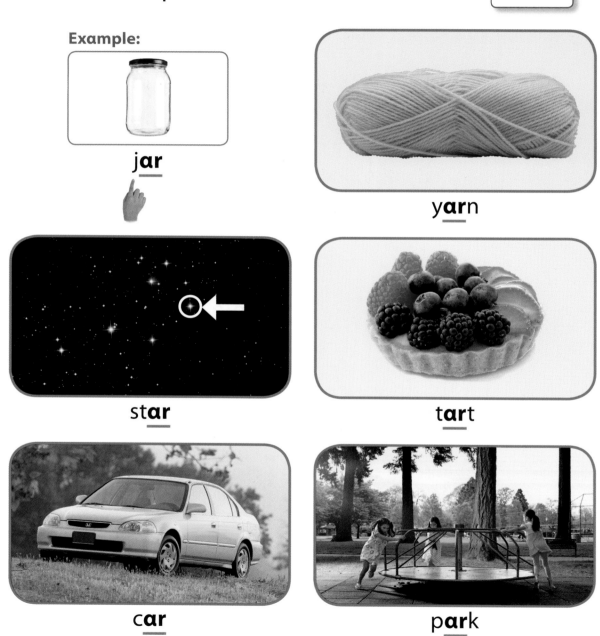

Example:

j**ar**

y**ar**n

st**ar**

t**ar**t

c**ar**

p**ar**k

Key Words

Look at the pictures and read the sentences. Then answer the question.

High Frequency Words
before
could
people
today
warm
were

Stars in the Sky

1. Stars **were** in the sky long **before** **today**.
2. In time, **people** used tools to look at stars.
3. These tools **could** help people see more stars.
4. One star keeps us **warm**. What star is it?

Hint: We see this star in daytime.

Phonics Games
NGReach.com

Answer: The sun

3

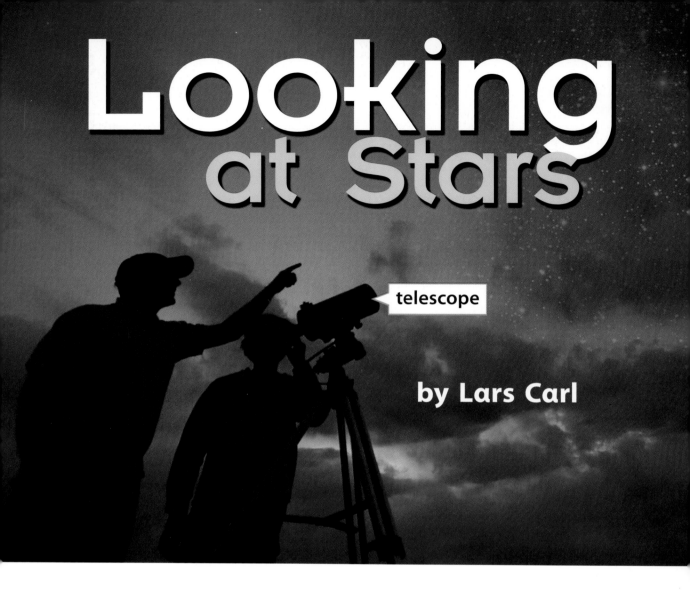

Looking at Stars

telescope

by Lars Carl

What are these people looking at? They are looking at the stars in the dark sky. The stars are far away. The bright stars shine like sparks of light.

One of the people has a telescope.

What is a telescope? A telescope is a tool. Many things seem small when they are far away. Small things can be hard to see. A telescope makes things look large.

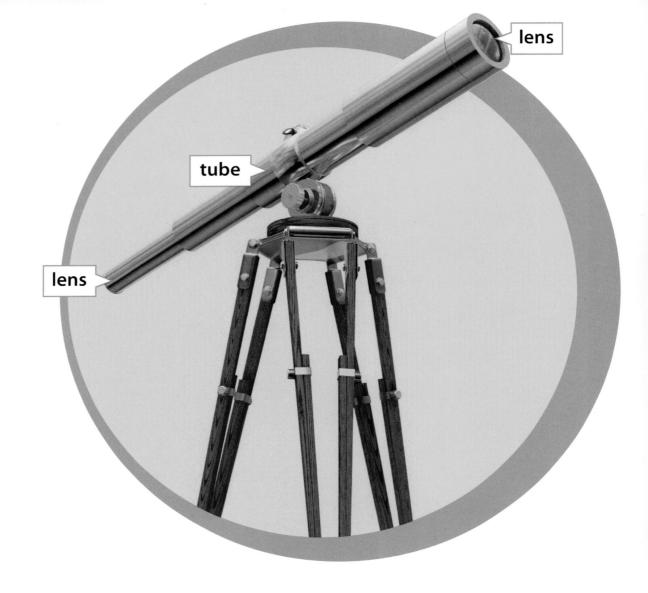

Look at the parts of this telescope. The tube is the main part. Glass lenses are at each end. They collect light to help you see with the telescope.

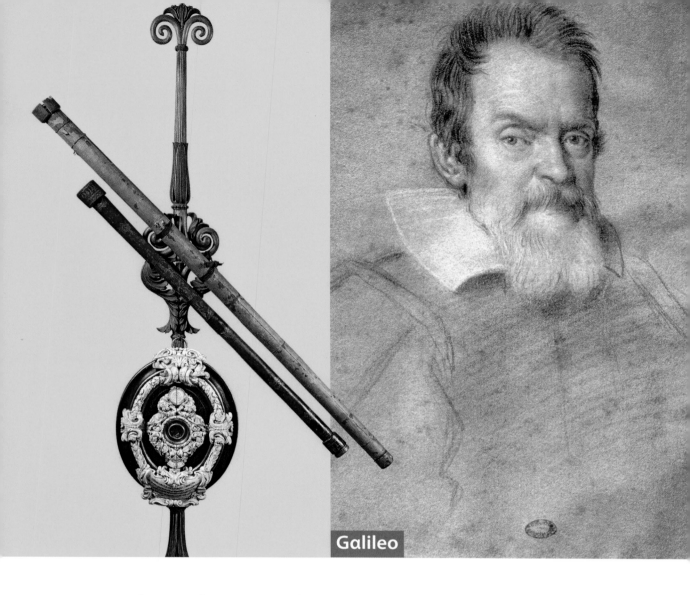

Galileo

What do you think this is? It is a telescope. A smart man named Galileo made it in 1609. He made it to look at the night sky.

7

1608
People first use telescopes.

1609
Galileo makes his first telescope.

Galileo was the first man to use a telescope to look at the night sky. He could see things he had not seen before. Soon other people were using telescopes to look at the sky.

old

new

Today people still use telescopes to look at the sky. Look at the old and the new telescopes on this page. How are they the same?

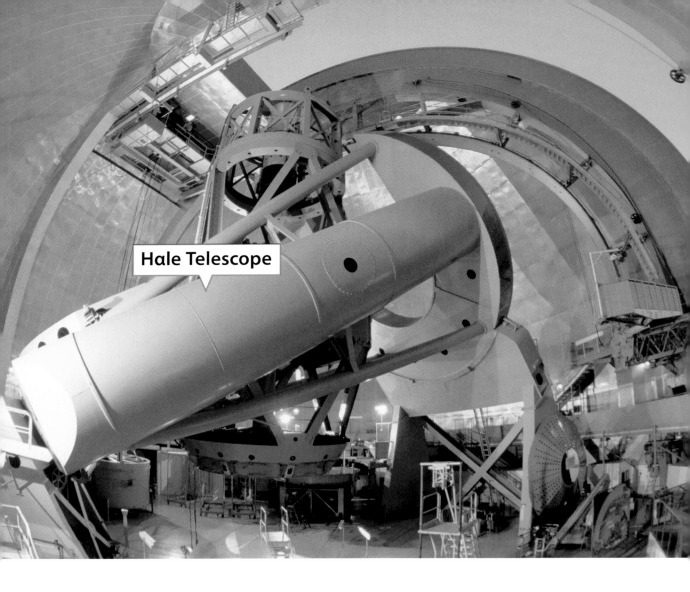

Today we use some LARGE telescopes.

The Hale Telescope is one of them.

Today we can send telescopes into space! This telescope is in space. It helps us see what space is like.

photo of Mars

A telescope in space took this photo of Mars. Mars is far away in space. The photo lets us see what Mars looks like. Telescopes are good tools! ❖

Words with <u>ar</u>

Read these words.

stars	plants	sky	yard	dark
sparks	large	barn	trees	hay

Find the words with **ar**.
Use letters to build them.

s	t	a	r	s

Talk Together

I see _stars_ in the _sky_.

Choose words from the box above to tell your partner about each place.

1.

2.

3.

Words with **kn, wr, gn, mb**

Look at each picture. Read the words.

Example:

knot

wrench

gnome

si**gn**

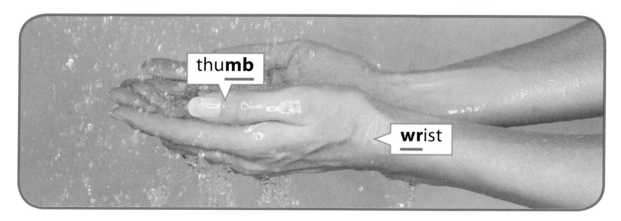

thu**mb**

wrist

High Frequency
Words

| before |
| could |
| people |
| today |
| warm |
| were |

Key Words

Look at the pictures. Read the sentences.

Stars Help Living Things

1. Long **before** **today**, stars **were** helping us.

2. Stars helped **people** keep from getting lost.

3. People **could** use stars to find their way.

4. The sun is also a star. It keeps people and plants **warm**.

The sun is a <u>very</u> warm star!

Phonics Games

NGReach.com

15

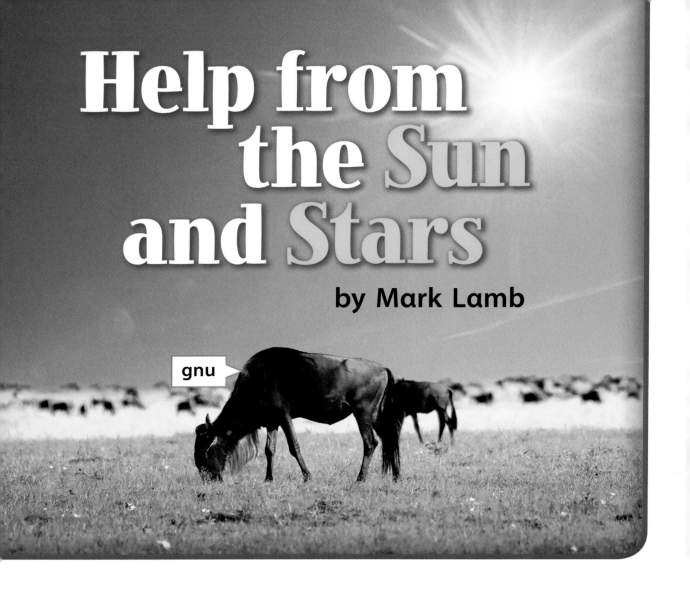

Help from the Sun and Stars

by Mark Lamb

gnu

The sun is a star. It helps us a lot. The sun helps plants grow. People eat plants. So do animals, such as this gnu.

crops

ice

The Sun Helps Plants Grow in the Cold

We grow some plants for food.
Snow and ice wreck these plants.
When it is too cold, people cannot
grow crops outside.

17

glass greenhouse

Long before today, people knew
that plants needed to be warm. They
knew that plants needed light. So people
started to grow plants in greenhouses.
Many greenhouses were made of glass.

18

hoop

plastic

plastic greenhouse

Today, greenhouses may be plastic. Some look like hoops wrapped with plastic. The sun shines in and helps heat the greenhouses. With greenhouses and the sun, we can grow plants in the cold.

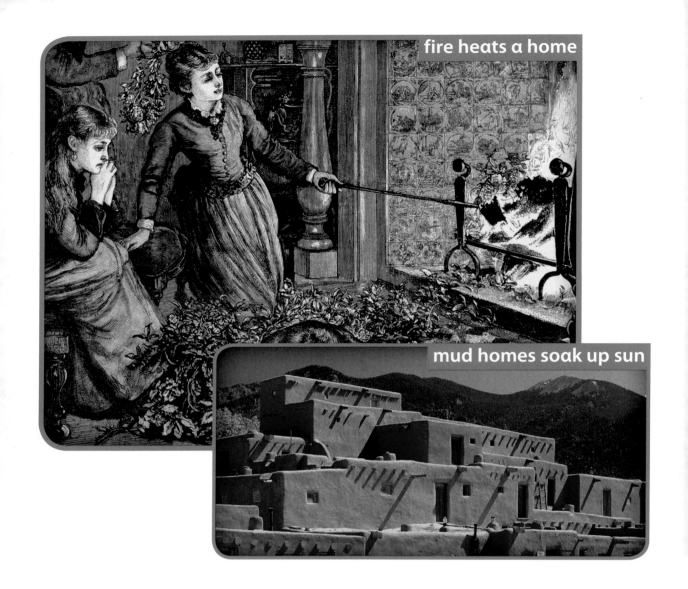

fire heats a home

mud homes soak up sun

The Sun Helps Us Live in the Cold

On a cold day, people can turn on the heat or make a fire in their homes. But homes can warm themselves! Homes made of mud bake in the sun, soaking up the warm rays.

roof

Today, people have other ways to make the sun warm their homes. The roof on this home traps the sun's heat.

People use the sun to heat barns, too. This warm barn is a safe place for these lambs and sheep.

sailors

The Sun and Stars Show the Way

The sun and the stars help keep people safe, too. Long before today, people wrote that sailors could use the sun and stars to find their way at sea.

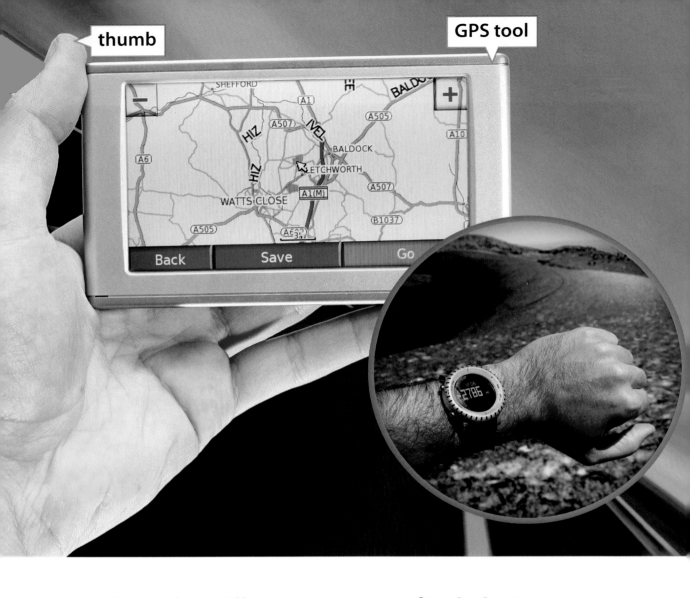

thumb

GPS tool

SHEFFORD • A1 • BALDO • HIZ • A507 • IVE • A505 • A10 • A6 • BALDOCK • LETCHWORTH • A507 • WATTS CLOSE • A1(M) • A505 • A5?? • B1037

Back   Save   Go

2786

People still use stars to find their way.

They can use tools, too, such as a GPS tool.

A GPS tool lets you know where you are.

Some people have a GPS tool in their watch.

One day a GPS tool may fit on a thumb! ❖

Words with <u>kn</u>, <u>wr</u>, <u>gn</u>, <u>mb</u>

Read these words.

know	knees	way	lambs	plants
wrecks	grows	gnome	thumbs	wrist

Find the words with **kn**, **wr**, **gn**, or **mb**. Use letters to build them.

k n o w

The sun keeps <u>thumbs</u> warm.

Talk Together

Choose words from the box above to complete the sentence. Tell your partner how the sun helps living things.

Get to the Barn Before It's Dark!

Pick! Be a lamb or a gnu.

Put a marker on START. Take turns.

Roll the dice.

Move your marker. Read the clues.

thumb

wrist

START

It's warm and sunny today.

Go 2 more.

Could you tell me where my tart is?

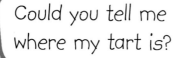

gnome

It is far to the barn. Hurry!

Go 2 more.

TART

26

star

Do gnus and lambs live on farms? Yes!

Go 2 more.

It's getting dark! How many stars do you see?

People are going to sleep. Hurry!

Go 1 more.

People have wrists and thumbs. Do lambs and gnus? No!

There is a knot in the garden hose.

Go back 1.

knot

Were you the first one here? Are you the gnu or the lamb?

You find a large jar. What could you put in it?

barn

jar

Acknowledgments

Grateful acknowledgment is given to the authors, artists, photographers, museums, publishers, and agents for permission to reprint copyrighted material. Every effort has been made to secure the appropriate permission. If any omissions have been made or if corrections are required, please contact the Publisher.

Photographic Credits

CVR (Cover) Topic Photo Agency/age fotostock. **2** (bl) Artville. (br) Todd Warnock/Getty Images. (cl) Paul LeFevre/iStockphoto. (cr) Sharon Day/iStockphoto. (tl) mm88/iStockphoto. (tr) Stockbyte/Getty Images. **3** (bl) Jose Luis Pelaez, Inc./Blend Images/Corbis. (cl) Steve Cole/iStockphoto. (r) Liz Garza Williams/Hampton-Brown/National Geographic School Publishing. (tl) The Print Collector/Alamy Images. **4** (l) Erik Isakson/Tetra Images/Jupiterimages. **4-5** (bg) Ekaterina Starshaya/Shutterstock. **6** James Steidl/Shutterstock. **7** (l) Superstock/Photolibrary. (r) Ottavio Mario Leoni/Getty Images. **8** Bettmann/Corbis. **9** (l) Jody Dole/Getty Images. (r) 3dimentii/Shutterstock. **10** Roger Ressmeyer/Corbis. **11** (bg) DigitalStock/Corbis. (fg) NASA/National Geographic Image Collection. **12** (bg) Steven J. Kazlowski/Alamy Images. (inset) NASA/National Geographic Image Collection. **13** (bc) Joshua Haviv/iStockphoto. (bl) Eyebyte/Alamy Images. (br) Maria Dryfhout/Shutterstock. (t) Liz Garza Williams/Hampton-Brown/National Geographic School Publishing. **14** (b) Christopher Thomas/Jupiterimages. (cl) Tom Young/iStockphoto. (cr) PhotoDisc/Getty Images. (tl) Tomas Bercic/iStockphoto. (tr) PhotoDisc/Getty Images. **15** (b) Liz Garza Williams/Hampton-Brown/National Geographic School Publishing. (tl) North Wind Picture Archives/Alamy Images. (tr) laurent dambies/iStockphoto. **16** stefanie van der vinden/iStockphoto. **17** Wayne Eastep/Getty Images. **18** Alinari Archives/Corbis. (fg) Stockbyte/Getty Images. **19** Oleksiy Maksymenko/Alamy Images. **20** (b) Comstock/Jupiterimages. (t) Bettmann/Corbis. **21** OxfordSquare/Shutterstock. **22** (bg) Wayne Hutchinson/AgStockUSA. (fg) PhotoDisc/Getty Images. **23** The Granger Collection, New York. **24** (bg) Olaru Radian-Alexandru/Shutterstock. (inset) Sebastien Cote/iStockphoto. **25** (bl) Amy Myers/iStockphoto. (br) Eric Gevaert/Alamy Images. (t) Liz Garza Williams/Hampton-Brown/National Geographic School Publishing.

Illustrator Credits

26-27 Alessia Girasole

The National Geographic Society

John M. Fahey, Jr., President & Chief Executive Officer
Gilbert M. Grosvenor, Chairman of the Board

Copyright © 2011 The Hampton-Brown Company, Inc., a wholly owned subsidiary of the National Geographic Society, publishing under the imprints National Geographic School Publishing and Hampton-Brown.

All rights reserved. No part of this book may be reproduced or transmitted in any form or by any means, electronic or mechanical, including photocopying, recording, or by an information storage and retrieval system, without permission in writing from the Publisher.

National Geographic and the Yellow Border are registered trademarks of the National Geographic Society.

National Geographic School Publishing
Hampton-Brown
www.NGSP.com

Printed in the USA.
RR Donnelley, Jefferson City, MO

ISBN: 978-0-7362-8046-4

12 13 14 15 16 17 18 19
10 9 8 7 6 5 4

New High Frequency Words

before
could
people
today
warm
were

Target Sound/Spellings

r-Controlled Vowel a̲r̲	Silent Consonants k̲n̲, w̲r̲, g̲n̲, m̲b̲
Selection: Looking at Stars	**Selection: Help from the Sun and Stars**
dark	gnu
far	knew
hard	know
large	lamb(s)
Mars	thumb
part	wrapped
smart	wreck
sparks	wrote
star(s)